THE DRUG ENFORCEMENT ADMINISTRATION

Rescue and Prevention: Defending Our Nation

- Biological and Germ Warfare Protection
- Border and Immigration Control
- Counterterrorist Forces with the CIA
- The Department of Homeland Security
- The Drug Enforcement Administration
- Firefighters
- Hostage Rescue with the FBI
- The National Guard
- Police Crime Prevention
- Protecting the Nation with the U.S. Air Force
- Protecting the Nation with the U.S. Army
- Protecting the Nation with the U.S. Navy
- Rescue at Sea with the U.S. and Canadian Coast Guards
- The U.S. Transportation Security Administration
- Wilderness Rescue with the U.S. Search and Rescue Task Force

RESCUE AND PREVENTION: Defending Our Nation

THE DRUG ENFORCEMENT ADMINISTRATION

CLIVE SOMERVILLE

MASON CREST PUBLISHERS
www.masoncrest.com

Mason Crest Publishers Inc.
370 Reed Road
Broomall, PA 19008
(866) MCP-BOOK (toll free)
www.masoncrest.com

First printing

1 2 3 4 5 6 7 8 9 10

Library of Congress Cataloging-in-Publication Data on file
at the Library of Congress

ISBN 1-59084-413-0

Editorial and design by
Amber Books Ltd.
Bradley's Close
74–77 White Lion Street
London N1 9PF
www.amberbooks.co.uk

Project Editor: Michael Spilling
Design: Graham Curd
Picture Research: Natasha Jones

Printed and bound in Jordan

Picture credits
DEA Museum, Washington, D.C.: 10, 36, 42; Encompass Graphics: 41; Popperfoto: 8, 12, 17, 27, 29, 30, 53, 57, 59, 60, 63, 65, 69, 70, 74; Topham Picturepoint: 6, 13, 14–15, 18, 20, 22, 24, 32, 35, 39, 45, 47, 48, 54, 64, 66, 72, 73, 76, 79, 80, 83, 84, 86, 87, 88, 89.
Front cover: Popperfoto, DEA Museum (top left).

DEDICATION

This book is dedicated to those who perished in the terrorist attacks of September 11, 2001, and to all the committed individuals who continually serve to defend freedom and protect the American people.

CONTENTS

INTRODUCTION

September 11, 2001, saw terrorism cast its lethal shadow across the globe. The deaths inflicted at the Twin Towers, at the Pentagon, and in Pennsylvania were truly an attack on the world and civilization itself. However, even as the impact echoed around the world, the forces of decency were fighting back: Americans drew inspiration from a new breed of previously unsung, everyday heroes. Amid the smoking rubble, firefighters, police officers, search-and-rescue, and other "first responders" made history. The sacrifices made that day will never be forgotten.

Out of the horror and destruction, we have fought back on every front. When the terrorists struck, their target was not just the United States, but also the values that the American people share with others all over the world who cherish freedom. Country by country, region by region, state by state, we have strengthened our public-safety efforts to make it much more difficult for terrorists.

Others have come to the forefront: from the Coast Guard to the Border Patrol, a wide range of agencies work day and night for our protection. Before the terrorist attacks of September 11, 2001, launched them into the spotlight, the courage of these guardians went largely unrecognized, although in truth, the sense of service was always honor enough for them. We can never repay the debt we owe them, but by increasing our understanding of the work they do, the *Rescue and Prevention: Defending Our Nation* books will enable us to better appreciate our brave defenders.

Steven L. Labov—CISM, MSO, CERT 3
Chief of Department, United States Search and Rescue Task Force

Left: Members of the Colombian anitdrug squad walk through a field of poppies, which are used to make deadly heroin.

WHAT IS THE DEA?

The DEA, or Drug Enforcement Administration, is the drug-busting arm of the Department of Justice, and is responsible for carrying out the drug laws and regulations of the United States, laid down by the Office of National Drug Control Policy (ONDCP). The DEA's role is to enforce these laws, bringing illegal drug dealers and manufacturers to justice.

This, of course, includes working to reduce the amount of drugs finding their way into the United States from foreign countries. Drugs are a danger whether produced at home or abroad. Indeed, the DEA's mission statement makes this explicit:

"The mission of the Drug Enforcement Administration (DEA) is to enforce the controlled-substances laws and regulations of the United States and bring to the criminal and civil justice system of the United States, or any other competent jurisdiction, those organizations and principal members of organizations involved in the growing, manufacture, or distribution of controlled substances appearing in or destined for illicit traffic in the United States; and to recommend and support non-enforcement programs aimed at reducing the availability of illicit controlled substances on the domestic and international markets."

Left: The Drug Enforcement Agency seizes huge amounts of drugs every year, destroying them before they can harm American and other citizens.

Ready for action, DEA agents receive first-class firearms training to protect U.S. citizens from the heavily armed gangs of the drug world.

HOW THE DEA IS ORGANIZED

The DEA employs over 9,000 people, and has a federal budget of $1.66 billion. It works with state, federal, and foreign agencies to spread these resources in the worldwide battle against drugs.

More than half of its staff (4,600) are Special Agents, responsible for tackling drugs on the ground. Other personnel include 500 diversion investigators, 700 intelligence specialists, 260 forensic chemists, and over 3,000 administrative and technical-support staff. In charge of it all is DEA Administrator Asa Hutchinson.

Asa Hutchinson became administrator of the DEA on August 8, 2001. Prior to this, he had been a lawyer for 21 years, and was just 31 years old when President Reagan appointed him U.S. Attorney for West Arkansas—the youngest U.S. Attorney in the nation.

During that time, he negotiated a peaceful end to a standoff with a heavily armed terrorist group in Northern Arkansas, and successfully prosecuted its members on **racketeering** charges. Later, as a congressman, he served on the Speaker's Task Force for a Drug-Free America, working to find ways of reducing drug use among young Americans. He went on to play a mediating role in the impeachment trial of President Clinton in 2000, and was praised for his diplomatic skills. As head of the DEA, he has recognized the need to reduce both drug supply and drug demand, encouraging effective enforcement strategies alongside better drug-education programs.

COMBATING DRUGS

Combining several strategies to carry out its mission, the DEA seeks to bring to justice powerful national and international drug dealers, as well as drug gangs, who use fear and violence to terrorize people in their communities. The DEA also works with state, federal, and foreign agencies to investigate those making and supplying drugs and bring them to justice. It helps these agencies destroy illegal drug laboratories and illegal drug crops, seeking to replace these with legal crops. And the DEA trains foreign agencies to deal with drugs in their own countries. This all helps reduce the amount of drugs supplied to the United States.

The DEA seizes the **assets** of drug dealers, such as money, cars, boats, and houses, to prevent them from carrying on their activities. It also runs community programs to help users kick the habit and educate younger people about the dangers of drugs to discourage them from using drugs before they ever start.

A Colombian coca plant, which was used to make cocaine, is displayed by a local farmer. His hat proudly displays the DEA logo.

Throughout this book, you will see how the DEA puts these methods into practice, and learn how its high-tech methods and constant vigilance is winning the war on drugs.

THE PROBLEM WITH DRUGS

You may have heard people your own age say they have taken drugs. They usually start because of peer pressure. Someone in their group of friends suggests they try it and—not wanting to look different or scared—they join in. If they are honest, most people's first experience of drugs is not pleasant. They may cough violently, choke, and have watery eyes or a runny nose. But if they keep taking it, their body learns to tolerate the drug, and eventually to crave it until they cannot do without it. In other words, they become addicted. They may also begin to enjoy the effects of the drugs, many of which produce feelings of excitement, **euphoria**, or even **hallucinations**, but only for a short time.

Meanwhile, these drugs are damaging the body. Gradually, the users' physical and mental powers become weaker and weaker, and they feel ill and confused most of the time. Family and friends may

Helicopters are a vital weapon in the war against drugs, spying on drug plantations and landing drug-enforcement teams in difficult terrain. Here, a Colombian antidrug team carries out a raid on a remote coca plantation in southern Colombia.

SUMMARY OF DANGEROUS DRUGS

DRUG	ALSO KNOWN AS...	EFFECT	WHAT IS IT MADE FROM AND HOW IS IT TAKEN?
MARIJUANA	Pot, Grass, Weed, Reefer, Acapulco Gold, Mary Jane	Sedative/Depressant	Dried leaves and tops of the cannabis plant, smoked in cigarettes or eaten.
COCAINE	Coke, Flake, Snow, Crack	Stimulant (the most potent natural stimulant known)	A fine white powder, made from the coca plant, sniffed, smoked, injected, or eaten.
HEROIN	Horse, Smack	Sedative/Depressant	A white powder with a bitter taste, made from the opium poppy plant. Injected or smoked.
ECSTASY	MDMA, XTC	Stimulant/ Hallucinogenic	A combination of chemicals swallowed as a tablet.
INHALANTS	Various solvents found in glue, hairspray, lighter fluid, paints, ands other household items	Stimulant	Solvents are inhaled from a soaked rag, sometimes from inside a bag, held to the face.
ROHYPNOL®	Flunitrazepam, Roofies, Date rape drug	Sedative	Tablets, available legally outside the U.S. to treat imsomnia.
METHAMPHETAMINE	Speed, Ice, Crystal, Meth	Stimulant	Chemicals formed into a white powder or rock-like crystals. Smoked, eaten, or injected.
LSD (Lysergic Acid Diethylamide)	Acid, Tabs, Microdots, Trips, Blotter, Cid, Doses. (There are over 80 street names.)	Hallucinogenic (the strongest known)	Chemicals diluted into a liquid, soaked onto quarter-inch square tabs of blotting paper (tabs) or sugar cubes, and eaten. Also made in tablet form (microdots).

WHY DO PEOPLE TAKE IT?	WHAT ARE THE DANGERS OF TAKING IT?	IS IT ADDICTIVE?
Relaxed feeling of well-being, disorientation, and sometimes hallucinations.	Fatigue, hunger, paranoia, lack of coordination, possible paranoia, risk of smoking-related diseases such as lung cancer and heart disease, risk to immune system.	Possibly
Increased awareness, hyperactivity, euphoria, disorientation; may cause hallucinations.	Anxiety; irritability; increased body temperature, blood pressure and pulse rate; insomnia; internal and nasal bleeding; appetite loss. Overdose can cause heart failure, hemorrhaging, and death.	Yes
Euphoria, drowsiness, overwhelming sense of well-being.	Watery eyes, runny nose, clammy skin, fatigue, appetite loss, irritability, panic, chills, cramps, nausea, and depression. Risk of HIV from infected needles. Overdose can cause shallow breathing, convulsions, coma, and death.	Yes
Hyperactivity, extreme sense of well-being and empathy for others.	Nausea, chills, paranoia, blurred vision, teeth clenching, rise in body temperature. Possible sleep and memory loss and emotional instability from brain damage. Overdose can cause death by heart failure and/or heat stroke.	Possibly
Similar to alcohol—feelings of well-being and dizziness.	Headaches, vomiting, wheezing, skin rashes, hearing loss, brain and organ damage, lung damage causing suffocation and death.	Possibly
Drowsiness, amnesia, loss of inhibitions; enhances other drugs such as heroin, cocaine, and alcohol.	Lethargy, dizziness, lack of coordination, confusion, amnesia, stomach problems.	Yes
Increased alertness, euphoria, a false sense of increased energy levels.	Apathy, fatigue, depression, irritability, violent/erratic behavior, paranoia, schizophrenia, increased blood pressure and pulse rate. An overdose can cause convulsions and possible death.	Yes—over-use leads to cravings to reach the previous "high," which cannot be achieved.
Powerful illusions and hallucinations. Altered perception of time, distance, color, sound, and touch.	Nausea, lower body temperature, sweating, rapid heart rate, mood swings. May also experience flashbacks of previous hallucinations, even months later. Overdose can lead to intense trips, psychosis, and death.	Not known

find it hard to recognize them. Eventually, the drugs could kill their users; indeed, it is all-too-easy to take an overdose by mistake.

And, of course, drugs cost money, a lot of money. When their own money runs out, drug users have to find the money elsewhere—by stealing from family and friends, or even robbing or mugging people in the street. And if a user owes a drug dealer money, he will not wait. First, he threatens; then he attacks to get his money, and it may not be the user he attacks, but his family. Soon, the drug user is simply trying to survive.

Chances are that others are also running scared. Drug dealers threaten entire communities, menacing users and fighting other drug gangs. Violent turf wars erupt as different gangs battle to take over a neighborhood, or to protect the one they control. Guns come out, and innocent people get killed. And what was once a safe community—the kind of place where children could play in the street safely and parents did not worry if children are gone a bit longer than they said they would be—is destroyed, the security replaced by violence and terror.

Figures prove that where the DEA has stopped a drug gang from operating in a community, both gun-related violence and the overall crime rate drop dramatically. Why? Because much of the violence and crime in communities is drug-related.

Moreover, that violence can extend nationwide, even worldwide.

Right: "What am I doing?" Drugs can really screw you up. Does smoking marijuana in a pile of trash really look like fun? Once addicted, the drug habit is difficult to lose.

If you hang out with the wrong crowd, do not be fooled that drugs are cool—they can kill. If your friends say try it, just say NO.

It is probable that the terrorist attacks of September 11, 2001, were funded by drugs. Osama bin Laden's Al Qaeda terrorist network gets much of its funding from drug **trafficking**, and many of these drugs are sold in the United States and Europe. There has never

DRUG USE AMONG THE 12–17 AGE GROUP:

Marijuana: The most frequently used illegal drug. In a 1999 survey by the National Center on Addiction and Substance Abuse, almost half (49.7%) of high school seniors said they had tried it at least once, and almost 10% of children were current users. Nearly half (49%) of teenagers said they had first experienced it at age 13, and half of all 13-year-olds agreed they could find and buy marijuana.

Cocaine: Usage among this age group is currently small, around 1.2%, but it is increasing. More of a threat to this age group is crack cocaine (crack), which is mixed with baking soda to make it smokable. This crackles when burned, hence the name. It is sold in small, cheap amounts, making it more attractive to the young.

Inhalants: Solvent abuse is common among young people, because the chemicals are easily available and easy to hide. A 1998 survey by the National Parents' Resource Institute for Drug Education found 2.2% of fourth graders admitted to sniffing solvents at least once a month. The dangers of inhalants were highlighted in 1999, when four high school girls killed in a Philadelphia car crash were found to have been sniffing a cleaning solvent.

been a better reason to just say no to drugs—and help in the war against terrorism.

All this explains why the DEA is working tirelessly to stamp out drugs, and why we should always say no. It is the smart thing to do.

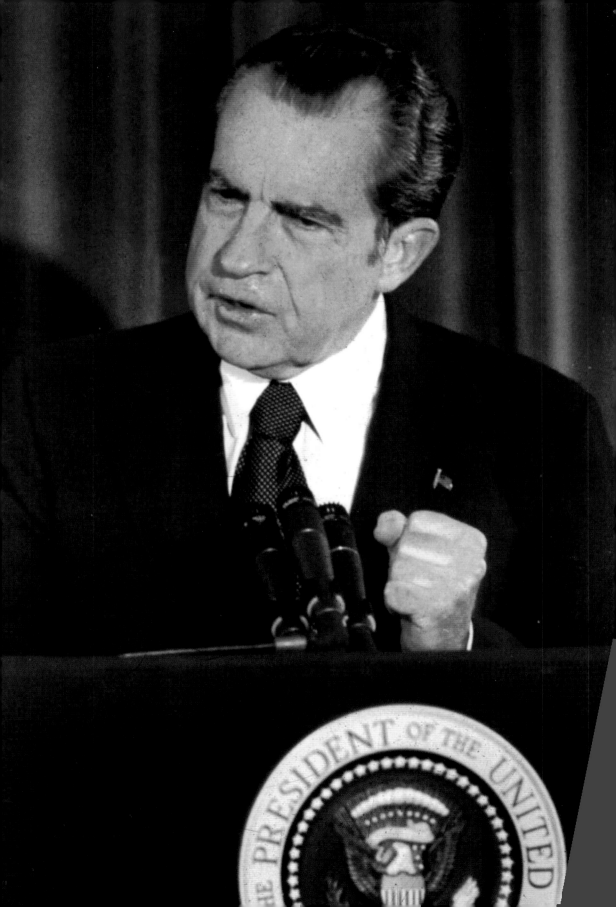

THE HISTORY OF THE DEA

The Drug Enforcement Administration was established in 1973 by President Nixon as a way of combining all the necessary government resources into one, effective, drug-fighting force. This move indicated that the government recognized drugs to be a growing threat to the United States.

In the 1960s, drugs were tolerated as a means of recreation, and **marijuana**, **cocaine**, and **LSD** had been particularly popular. But to understand the DEA of today, we need to go back in time to see how the drug problem in the United States began and how the government's attempts to tackle it led to the creation of the DEA. Looking at the development of the DEA since 1973 also provides a fascinating insight into how the administration has had to adapt to the changing drug culture over the decades.

THE ORIGINS OF THE DRUG PROBLEM

Drug abuse has been in the United States since the 19th century, when Americans discovered morphine, heroin, and cocaine. At first, these were used for medical purposes. At a time when medical knowledge was quite primitive, they were seen as wonder drugs because of their **anesthetic** effects. But users soon discovered these

Left: In 1973, President Nixon told America that it was time for the Drug Enforcement Administration to go to work in "an all-out global war on the drug menace."

drugs were a curse, not a salvation, for they became **addicts**. Added to this, opium dens were springing up all over the United States as Americans embraced the culture of the Chinese immigrants, who came to work in the gold mines and railroads in the 1850s. In a sense, the country suffered its first drug epidemic between 1850 and the start of World War I in 1914.

By the early 20th century, the government began to crack down on drugs. Indeed, the United States became one of the first countries to restrict drugs to medical use only. This, in turn, helped the

Many U.S. citizens embraced the Chinese opium dens of 19th-century America, causing the country to suffer its first drug epidemic.

Chinese government restrict the opium trade and limited the growing of coca crops, from which cocaine is made. The United States helped create international drug regulations and passed antidrug laws at home, too, laying the foundations for comprehensive drug enforcement.

In the 1920s, even alcohol was classified as an illegal drug. The era of Prohibition was known for gangsters like Al Capone, and between 1915 and 1927, drug enforcement was initially handled by the Internal Revenue Service (IRS).

The drug enforcement strategies of these forerunners of the DEA were successful in persuading society to turn away from illegal drugs, and by the start of World War II in 1939, the problem looked close to solved.

SWINGING SIXTIES

However, drug abuse reared its ugly head again with the hippie culture of the 1960s, as drugs like marijuana, cocaine, LSD, and amphetamines became popular. This new generation actively encouraged drug taking, which they saw as a way to "expand" their minds and rebel against the conventions of society. The drug problem reached epidemic proportions again, and a drug culture was threatening to dominate the country. The range of drugs was growing, highly dangerous hallucinogens and **amphetamines** were becoming increasingly popular, and a whole generation of drug users were now becoming drug dealers, too.

By the end of the 1960s, the government had no doubt that drastic measures had to be taken against drugs. Congress passed the

Controlled Substances Act (CSA) in 1970. This replaced over 50 previous drug laws, and was an attempt to combine the multitude of drug regulations into one nationwide policy. Now all that was needed was a central agency to enforce it, free of the bureaucratic rivalries that existed between the current government agencies. So in 1973, President Nixon combined the government's drug enforcement resources into one agency, and the Drug Enforcement Administration was born, tasked by the president to lead an "all-out global war on the drug menace."

THE DEA THROUGH THE DECADES
1970s: The Cocaine Years

In many ways, the DEA faced its toughest task in its first 10 years. Drug abuse reached a peak in 1979, with a shocking 1 in 10 Americans using drugs regularly. Particularly popular was cocaine, seen as an expensive, harmless, "high-society" drug. As more people used cocaine, however, the supply increased, mainly from the powerful Medillin **cartel** in Colombia. As the supply increased, the price dropped, until by the middle of the 1980s, more than six million people were using it. The drug, therefore, lost its "exclusive-lifestyle" tag, and by the 1980s, dealers were looking for a new market—they soon found it.

Left: Tune in and drop out: communal events like rock festivals encouraged drug taking in the 1960s, 1970s, and 1980s. By 1979, drug abuse reached its peak: 1 in 10 Americans used them on a regular basis.

The other drug popular in the 1970s was **heroin**. However, the DEA scored big successes against heroin in this decade. The number of heroin addicts in the United States fell from 500,000 to 380,000; deaths caused by heroin dropped by 80 percent; and the DEA estimated that by 1981, there was 40 percent less heroin available than in 1976.

1980s: "Crack" and the Rise of the Drug Cartels

The cocaine boom of the 1970s established the Medillin cartel as the most powerful—and violent—drug syndicate in the world. Initially, the cartel was content to supply from its bases in Colombia, but now it began to infiltrate the United States so that it could control distribution of drugs within the country.

As the price of pure cocaine fell, its rich customers drifted away, so "crack" was developed, targeting the poorer, inner-city areas. Crack is simply cocaine combined with baking soda, formed into large crystals, or "rocks," and smoked. At that time, pure cocaine cost $100 per gram, but by 1985, a hit was available on the street for as little as $2.50. And it was highly addictive. Not surprisingly, demand among the poor and teenagers boomed, and the Medillin drug cartel became firmly established within the United States.

With the crack epidemic taking hold, the country suffered unprecedented levels of drug-related violence. In 1981, there were 621 murders in Miami, an increase of around 80 percent from 1979. Drugs became the primary concern across the United States, and in 1982, President Reagan intervened. The DEA was sent to Miami to form a joint task force with the Army, the FBI, and local

These Russian youths are playing with fire by heating heroin over a flame to prepare it for injecting. Dirty syringes, contaminated drugs, and the risk of overdosing make this a deadly game.

law enforcement officers. Their success in reducing drug-related crime led to similar DEA task forces set up elsewhere.

In 1988, 65 percent of the DEA's arrests were for cocaine. Seizures of the drug increased, too, from 440 lb (200 kg) in 1977, to 132,276 lb (60,000 kg) by 1988. The crack era was the worst drug epidemic in the nation's history, and, if it were not for the work of the DEA and other agencies, it could have produced a whole generation of crack addicts.

The decade also saw a major shift in DEA policy. From this point onward, the DEA has not just focused on enforcing domestic drug

THE CONTROLLED SUBSTANCES ACT

The 1970 Controlled Substances Act (CSA) was part of the Drug Abuse Prevention and Control Act, and replaced over 50 pieces of legislation with one, effective law. It entered the statute books on May 1, 1971. The act also set up a system of drug classification, by which all controlled and illegal substances are classified into one of five schedules, based on three factors: how dangerous they are, how addictive, and whether they actually have any medical value.

Schedule 1 is the most dangerous and includes marijuana, heroin, and LSD, with a sliding scale down to Schedule 5. For the first time in history, America had a single classification system for all types of controlled drugs, and when the DEA came into being two years later, the act gave it a vital foundation for its drug enforcement work.

laws. It has also pursued international drug organizations at home and abroad, seeking to destroy them and their evil trade.

1990s: The "Kingpin" Strategy and the Rise of Rave Culture

After the experience of the 1980s, the DEA initiated its "kingpin" strategy in 1992, which involved taking on the powerful drug syndicates by hitting them at their weakest point—their laboratories, chemicals, finances, and drug-trafficking infrastructure, both within the United States and abroad. After some ill-advised cuts in the

1980s, the DEA's funding was boosted in the 1990s, and 1992 brought its first billion-dollar budget—a far cry from the $700,000 it began with in 1973, and evidence of just how important its job had become.

The kingpin strategy produced results fast. Indeed, the DEA had achieved stunning successes by 1993, severely damaging the

A Mexican plainclothes policeman destroys opium poppies in the Mexican highlands with a pen knife before they can be harvested for heroin. The DEA cooperates closely with their counterparts in Central and South America to combat the drug trade at its source.

Medillin cartel's power base. They also worked with the Colombian National Police (CNP) to try and capture the murderous Medillin bosses, including the notorious Pablo Escobar, in their own backyard. That very same year, the DEA was proud to cross out Escobar's face from a wanted poster after he was shot dead by the CNP in a rooftop gun battle. The DEA has continued its successful kingpin strategy, taking on the sinister, but less violent, successors to the Medillins, the Cali cartel.

Mexican drug lords also increased their power in the '90s, diversifying into cocaine and heroin production. With cocaine, heroin, and marijuana still supplied in the United States in large quantities, the country was hit by a new threat in the mid 1990s—**ecstasy**, also known as XTC. This highly dangerous chemical drug has become increasingly popular among young people attending dance raves at open-air venues and nightclubs. Popular for its effects of increased alertness and euphoria desired at such occasions, its use increased by 500 percent between 1993 and 1998, costing around $25 a tablet.

The DEA saw seizures of the drug surge, from 200 tablets in 1993, to over 200,000 in 1999. If rave culture declines, it is hoped that use of XTC will follow suit. Meanwhile the DEA's proud tradition of drug enforcement continues into the new millennium.

Left: In August 1999, 60 airline employees were arrested at Miami International Airport in Operation Ramp Rats for smuggling drugs and weapons. Handcuffed, a man hangs his head as he is escorted away by DEA officers.

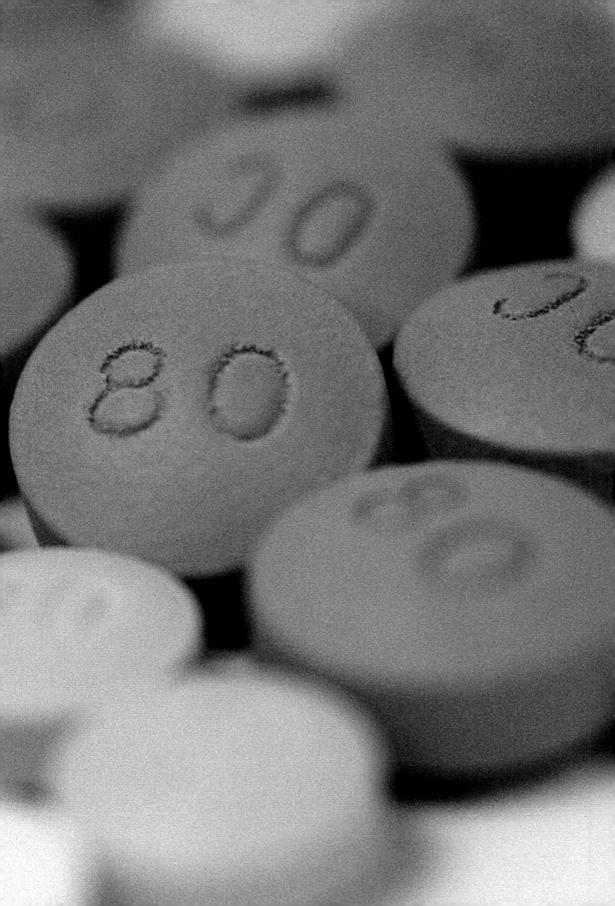

THE DEA AT HOME

The DEA works tirelessly to enforce federal drug laws and stamp out the supply of drugs to the United States. It is active on both a local and a national level, and has set up a number of operations and programs using dedicated teams to wage war on drugs.

The DEA is made up of specialized departments that work with each other and outside agencies to create a highly effective drug-fighting force. The Special Agents, who carry out drug enforcement on the front line, are backed up by a wide range of departments, personnel, and antidrug programs.

THE OFFICE OF INTELLIGENCE

To be successful, the DEA must know what its enemy is planning and stay one step ahead. Shortly after its creation in 1973, it established an Office of Intelligence to gather and assess three types of intelligence:

Tactical: Discover how illegal drugs are transported and by which groups and gangs.

Operational: Judge how efficient the structure of the DEA is and how successful its operations are so that improvements can be made and the agency can learn from experience.

Left: The most bitter of pills—the DEA works throughout America to keep "designer" drugs, such as these ecstasy tablets, off our streets and away from young people.

Strategic: Build up a picture of the whole drug-dealing system, from where the drugs are made to how they are processed, smuggled, and distributed throughout America.

The Office of Intelligence is staffed by specialist Intelligence Analysts (IAs) skilled in gathering and analyzing all sorts of information, from a dealer's coded telephone call, to data hidden on a notebook computer.

The Computer Forensics team, for example, is skilled at retrieving information from electronic devices, such as computers and personal organizers, seized from suspected drug dealers. IAs work mostly out in the field, often in mobile intelligence units linked by satellite, supporting the Special Agents in operations all over the United States. Their numbers have grown dramatically, from just 11 in 1974, to over 600 today, proving just what a vital role they play.

AN EPIC ACHIEVEMENT

The DEA's El Paso Intelligence Center (EPIC) was set up in 1974 to gather and analyze intelligence collected by the DEA and other agencies, mainly along the U.S. border with Mexico. It has now expanded into a national drug-intelligence center, acting as the focal point for drug information gathered by all U.S. law enforcement agencies, at home and abroad.

Just as the DEA was set up to combine drug enforcement agencies into one organization, so EPIC now coordinates all national drug intelligence under one roof. This helps to ensure that no vital information is lost.

Listening to the word on the street, DEA agents work alongside police to gather intelligence firsthand in our neighborhoods and feed it back to EPIC for analysis.

FORENSIC SCIENCE

The role of the forensic scientist is vital in the DEA. The scientists analyze drugs seized in DEA operations, as well as other forensic evidence, such as fingerprints, so that law enforcement agencies can build a case against drug dealers. They work in state-of-the-art laboratories that are the envy of the scientific world. From around 100 scientists in 1973, their numbers have almost tripled to around 300 today, and they handle hundreds of thousands of items a year. Some work in central laboratories, while others go out to field laboratories to assist agents on the front line.

LOCAL ACTION: CLEANING UP COMMUNITIES

The DEA has several teams that go out and work alongside local law enforcement agencies to cut off the supply of drugs at the final stage—in the community. By removing the neighborhood drug dealers, these teams can take away money from the drug lords who employ them and reduce the frightening level of drug-related violence and crime they cause. The teams offer essential backup to local law enforcement officers, who would otherwise be over-whelmed by the scale of drug dealing and drug-related crime in their town.

One of the DEA's most successful strategies has been the estab-lishment of Mobile Enforcement Teams (METs). The DEA created these in 1995 to help fight drug-related violent crime in communi-ties. They assist local law enforcement officers, including police chiefs, sheriffs, and state prosecutors, to identify drug gangs, then arrest and prosecute them.

The teams have experienced tremendous success in a dangerous and difficult environment. By August 2000, MET teams had completed 265 operations throughout the United States, from Alabama to Wyoming, and arrested more than 11,000 people. In these operational areas, assaults fell by 15 percent, robberies by 14 percent, and homicides by 16 percent. Throughout the United States as a whole, violent crime dropped by more than one quarter between 1993 and 1996—unthinkable just a decade before when

Left: DEA forensic chemists analyze evidence used to bring drug dealers to justice and remove them from our communities.

HOW THE DEA "MET" WITH SUCCESS

The MET program against local drug dealers has brought the DEA stunning successes. Here are just three examples:

Lynn, Massachusetts, May '95–November '96

A gang of Hell's Angels deals cocaine and methamphetamine, and fights violent turf wars. After an 18-month operation led by the Boston MET, a notorious Hell's Angel, Greg Domey, is arrested with 15 others. Within six months, assaults and robberies in Lynn drop by almost one-quarter, and homicides by three-quarters.

Collier County, Florida, November '95–February '97

In 1995, Collier County suffers a huge rise in drug-related violence. The cause is a turf war between two cocaine gangs, run by Jerry Sloan and Jose Nelson Santos. The MET catches Santos at home red-handed, converting cocaine into crack, and seizes nearly $70,000 and documents that lead to the arrests of his associates. Sloan's drug ring is also smashed, and a total of 73 arrests are made.

Coconino County, Arizona, July '98–March '99

The MET works with the Northern Arizona Street Crimes Task Force to bust the Colimas and Castillo organizations. Infiltrating the two gangs, the MET seizes seven drug laboratories, and thousands of dollars' worth of drugs. They also seize over $16,000 in cash and arrest the two ringleaders, Colimas and Castillo.

Seen making a bust in a downtown street, the DEA's Mobile Enforcement Teams (METs) work tirelessly in our communities to rid our streets of local drug dealers and the violent crime they cause. Here, officers arrest suspected drug dealers in Philadelphia, Pennsylvania.

nearly two people a day were killed in Miami. Not only does this prove the success of the METs, it shows that drugs and violent crime go hand in hand.

HIGH-INTENSITY DRUG TRAFFICKING AREAS (HIDTAS)

Established in 1990, the HIDTA program identifies major drug-trafficking areas throughout the United States so that trafficking can be systematically reduced in these areas. The idea is not only to benefit the HIDTA areas themselves, but also to decrease the supply of drugs from these areas to other parts of the country. Five HIDTAs were identified in 1990, and there are now over 30.

Almost 300 DEA Special Agents work on the program, with an annual budget of nearly $200 million. Like the METs, the HIDTA agents work hand in hand with local and national law enforcement agencies to achieve their aim. To be identified as an HIDTA, an area must be a major center for drug trafficking or manufacturing; have a harmful effect on other areas of the country; and have local law enforcement agencies already working on the problem, but in need of additional resources, such as DEA agents, to help tackle it.

THE NATIONAL DRUG POINTER INDEX (NDPIX)

Because the drug problem in the United States is nationwide, there is always the risk that agencies from different areas are unknowingly working on the same case and running duplicate operations. This is not only an expensive waste of time and resources, it could also put Special Agents in danger if their cover is blown unwittingly by another agent running his own operation. It was to counter such problems that the DEA set up the NDPIX system in 1997, to alert agents to similar cases investigated elsewhere. NDPIX makes use of the existing National Law Enforcement Telecommunications System (NLETS), the high-speed system that links law enforcement

The 1990 HIDTA program shows the main drug-trafficking areas in the U.S. In 1994, the Southwest Border Initiative (SWBI) was created to combat the threat posed by Mexican-based drug trafficking groups operating along the southwest border.

agencies nationwide. Details of a case under investigation are entered into the NDPIX computer system, and a list of possible duplicate investigations is displayed. The agent can then call the other investigators concerned, discuss the case, and possibly combine forces. NDPIX has proved hugely popular with enforcement agencies—by 2000, more than 86,000 investigations were entered into the system.

OPERATIONS PIPELINE AND CONVOY, 1984–PRESENT

By the early 1980s, drug organizations had set up their distribution networks within the United States. State troopers in New Mexico and New Jersey began uncovering increasing amounts of drugs and cash in private vehicles pulled over for minor traffic violations, especially along Interstates 40 and 95. It was obvious that U.S. highways

Here, a DEA pilot undergoes training using flight-simulation equipment. DEA pilots constantly upgrade their skills through rigorous training.

CATCHING THE BIG FISH

The DEA launched Operation Swordfish—so-called because it aimed to catch the "big fish" running the drug syndicates—in Miami in December 1980. Special Agents set up a fake money-laundering business called Dean International Investments Inc., in the hope of luring in drug organizations that needed to launder their drug money into "legal" businesses.

Using a go-between, the DEA persuaded several major drug dealers to use their services, and 18 months later had gathered so much hard evidence that 67 U.S. and Colombian members were convicted. They also siezed $800,000 in cash and assets, several tons of marijuana, and 220 lb (100 kg) of cocaine. Such was the success of Swordfish that the operation became the model for drug task forces nationwide.

were used to transport drugs throughout the country.

The troopers also noticed that drug traffickers often shared certain characteristics and methods, and they became skilled at spotting likely suspects, often just by their words and actions. In response, the DEA launched Operation Pipeline in 1984, the name taken from the apparent "drug pipeline" that transported drugs from Florida and the southwest border into the rest of the United States, and which sent millions of dollars from drug sales in the opposite direction. Pipeline enabled police officers from New Mexico and New Jersey to train other officers nationwide in their interview and search techniques.

In 1990, the DEA began Pipeline's sister operation, Convoy, to target commercial vehicles trafficking drugs. This involves long-term surveillance and undercover work, often at places such as truck stops and cargo areas. Convoy also trains DEA agents to drive commercial vehicles for undercover investigations and help local police with seizures of commercial vehicles on their highways.

Are these operations successful? The figures speak for themselves: between 1996 and 2000, more than 2,204,600 lb (1 million kg) of marijuana, and 294,314 lb (133,500 kg) of cocaine were seized by Pipeline and Convoy. In the same period, almost 2,205 lb (1,000 kg) of crack and 1,102 lb (500 kg) of heroin were found in vehicles, plus 9,920 lb (4,500 kg) of methamphetamine and a mighty $604 million in cash.

THE DOMESTIC CANNABIS ERADICATION AND SUPPRESSION PROGRAM (DCE/SP)

Marijuana is the most widely used drug in the United States, and the only major illegal drug grown here. The Domestic Cannabis Eradication and Suppression program began in 1979 and had been adopted by all 50 states by 1999. Operations included Wipe Out in 1990, which eradicated 90 percent of Hawaii's cannabis crop by targeted spraying of herbicides. Similar successes nationwide forced growers to move their crops indoors, but the DEA now has thermal imaging equipment, which detects the heat from the special lights used to grow cannabis indoors. In 1999, the DCE/SP was responsible for destroying 3.5 million cultivated outdoor plants and more than 200,000 indoor plants. The largest indoor seizure was in a

HIDE AND SEEK

Traffickers try all sorts of amazing ways to smuggle drugs. Not all succeed:

• In 1991, 1,000 lb (454 kg) of heroin from Southeast Asia was seized in San Francisco—the largest haul in U.S. history. The drugs were hidden inside cartons of produce bags imported from Taiwan and wrapped in birthday giftwrap.

• In St. Petersburg, Russia, in 1993, 1.1 tons of cocaine were seized, hidden in cans of corned beef hash. The drugs had come all the way from Colombia.

• In December 1991, 15 tons of cocaine were found hidden in cement posts in Miami and Texas, shipped from Venezuela.

• Since the late 1990s, cocaine has been found chemically combined into woodchip furniture and even enamel bathtubs—to be chemically extracted later.

This is part of a $12-million haul of heroin discovered hidden in bags of dog food by British customs officers. Almost 100 kilos of the drug were uncovered.

disused mine in Northern California in August 1993, in which over 3,000 plants were found, with an estimated value of between six and nine million dollars. It took 40 people more than two days to remove the five tons of high-tech cultivation equipment from the mine.

WASHING AWAY THE MONEY LAUNDERERS

Money laundering is the process of turning cash from illegal drug sales into legitimate money so that it cannot be detected. Traffickers are using increasingly sophisticated laundering methods to try and disguise their ill-gotten gains. Money is first "layered," meaning that it is moved from place to place through various businesses and bank accounts to obscure its trail. It is then collected at the other end as "clean" money. The anonymity that today's online banking provides has made it difficult to trace such money.

The DEA has, however, had some successes. **Stings**, such as Operation Dinero in 1994 and Operations Green Ice I and II in 1992 and 1995 set up fake money-laundering services to catch the money movers in the act. Dinero alone recovered three valuable paintings and $90 million. The DEA has also been successful in seizing other assets from drug lords, such as computers, cars, houses, and aircraft, which helps prevent drug lords from continuing their evil trade. Collectively, this procedure is known as **asset forfeiture** and has played a major part in destroying drug syndicates.

WATCHING THE DETECTIVES

Today's drug syndicates are highly sophisticated, using all the latest technology, from computers to high-speed vehicles to surveillance

Here, DEA officers destroy illegally grown marijuana plants discovered on a farm in a rural part of Maine.

equipment—money is no object. They often have greater resources than many of the countries in which they operate. Not only can they control their vast global drug empires, they can also watch the law enforcement agents watching them.

Many illegal organizations employ ex-intelligence officers to run their intelligence operations. They also employ skilled chemists, who have the role of developing ever-more devious ways of smuggling drugs. Such chemists have now found ways to chemically combine drugs into everyday objects, like furniture, and then chemically extract the drugs once they are safely across the border. The DEA must use all its resources to outwit the drug lords in this constant game of high-tech cat and mouse.

THE DEA ABROAD

The drug menace is not just happening at home—it is a world-wide problem. To protect the United States from drugs, the DEA needs to be proactive, cutting off the supply of drugs abroad before they reach our shores. This means that cooperation with foreign drug-enforcement agencies is vital.

The United States has been fighting drugs abroad ever since the DEA's predecessor, the Federal Bureau of Narcotics, sent two agents to Turkey and France in 1949 to help cut the supply of heroin. Today, the DEA has offices in 56 countries all over the world, helping the host countries wage war on drugs and combat the violence that goes with them. In its efforts to help, the DEA focuses on five strategies:

Gathering Intelligence

The DEA is one of the most highly respected intelligence gatherers in the world. It provides vital information to foreign law-enforcement agencies on where drugs are made, who trafficks them, and how they operate. It can even show how the money from drugs is laundered. In addition, Joint Information Coordination

Left: A Colombian drug enforcement officer stands guard as tons of captured heroin are destroyed on a bonfire. The DEA works alongside agencies abroad—especially in Mexico and Colombia—to cut off the supply of drugs at its source.

Centers (JICCs), focused mainly in the Caribbean and Central and South America, teach host nations how to gather their own intelligence, based on the DEA's EPIC (El Paso Intelligence Center) in the United States.

Building Relationships

The DEA continually builds strong relationships with trustworthy governments and law enforcement agencies abroad, first to encourage strong antidrug laws in those countries, and then to assist in the enforcement of those laws. A good working relationship is also vital in getting the cooperation of the host nation to bring the suspects to justice.

Joint Investigations

The DEA assists the investigations of the host nations by carrying out undercover work, analyzing drug seizures, interviewing witnesses, and following up leads. This can also help the United States bring drug lords to justice, with the host nation letting drug lords arrested on U.S. soil be **extradited** to their country of origin for trial. The more the DEA can encourage this, the more the drug barons will realize there is no place they can hide.

Promoting International Law

If drugs are an international problem, then the best method of enforcement is international law, so that drug traffickers will face justice wherever they go. For example, the International Drug Enforcement Conference (IDEC) brings together high-ranking law

HELP FROM ABOVE

The DEA's Aviation Operations Center at Fort Worth, Texas, provides air support over land and sea, including surveillance, supplies, and spraying of illegal plantations. As well as serving the DEA at home, the Office of Aviation (OA) has branches in Central and South America and the Caribbean. The highly skilled pilots are DEA Special Agents, thus enabling the OA to be a fully integrated part of the DEA's international mission. The office has grown from 24 aircraft and 41 pilots in 1973, to 95 aircraft and 117 pilots today. Unlucky drug traffickers have helped the cause, too: around 85 percent of the fleet is aircraft seized from them.

enforcement officials from all the Americas and the Caribbean to discuss drug-related issues and international law.

International Training

The DEA trains foreign police forces to tackle drugs at the DEA training center in Quantico, Virginia, and at training centers in the countries themselves.

THE DEA IN CENTRAL AND SOUTH AMERICA
Mexico

Not surprisingly, one of the busiest drug-trafficking routes into America is across the Mexican border. Multi-ton shipments of drugs, such as marijuana, heroin, and methamphetamine, are smuggled by Mexican drug lords, while the Colombians pay the smugglers to transport tons of cocaine.

In an effort to cut off this supply route, the DEA launched the South West Border Initiative (SWBI) in 1994. It aims to identify the ringleaders of the drug organizations and how they operate along the border by tapping their phones and communication systems. The DEA works in partnership with the FBI and U.S. Customs and law enforcement agencies on the American side of the border and with Mexican forces in Juarez, Tijuana, and Monterrey on the other.

The SWBI is a great example of how cross-border cooperation can tackle drugs. Operations Reciprocity, Zorro II, and Limelight all used court-approved wire tapping, controlled by SWBI agents. The combined haul of these Mexican operations was 48,500 lb (22,000 kg) of drugs, $35 million in cash and assets, and the arrest of 156 people. And as drug smuggling fell, so did the drug-related violence and corruption in the border towns.

Colombia

In many ways, the DEA has enjoyed even better relations with the Colombian authorities than with those in Mexico. This is essential for the DEA's success, because the United States does not have an extradition treaty with Colombia, so any capture and prosecution of Colombian drug lords must be on Colombian soil. The DEA has established excellent working relations with the Colombian National Police (CNP), leading to the eventual collapse of the world's most-feared drug syndicate, the Medillin cartel, in the early 1990s. The DEA was helped in this by the Colombian authorities'

Masked Mexican federal agents stand guard outside a suspected money-laundering center as part of the joint DEA-Mexican South West Border Initiative.

determination not to give in to the cartel's rising wave of terror, intimidation, and bribery. After a complex DEA-CNP operation, cartel boss Fabio Ochoa gave himself up to the CNP in December 1990, and his two brothers, Jorge Luis and Juan David, did the same in consecutive months. In the same month as Jorge's capture, the CNP shot dead the crime bosses' top assassin, David Ricardo Prosco Lopera, who had killed 50 Medillin policeman and the Colombian Minister of Justice in 1984.

But the work of the DEA cooperation force in Colombia is not done. The violent Medillin cartel was replaced by the more slippery Cali Mafia, who substituted violence with quiet **infiltration** of all parts of American society to control their drug distribution network in the United States. They continued to run huge shipments of cocaine into the United States and to launder millions of dollars back to their base in Colombia. Once again, however, the DEA joined forces with the CNP, aiding in the capture of the Cali's Rodriguez-Orejuala in 1995, and Pacho Herrera the following year, effectively ending the Cali's influence. Today, the Colombian

Colombian police raid the home of a drug baron. Improved, DEA-led enforcement measures have led to the capture of several key figures in Colombia's drug cartels.

cocaine industry remains a huge problem, but is much more divided, making it easier for the DEA and the CNP to pick off individual groups.

Operation Snowcap

Launched in 1994, Snowcap is the DEA's attempt to train forces in neighboring countries to tackle drug manufacture and trafficking themselves. DEA agents have set up training programs and accompanied foreign law-enforcement agents on drug-busting missions within those countries to show them improved enforcement methods. Although the scheme has been reduced in recent years due to the massive drain on DEA resources, Snowcap has continued in three key drug-producing countries: Colombia, Peru, and Bolivia. In Colombia especially, DEA agents, trained in jungle warfare, have been able to show Colombian forces how to locate and destroy illegal drug laboratories hidden in the jungle, severely damaging drug-syndicate supply lines.

THE DEA IN THE CARIBBEAN

With the success of the SWBI along the Mexican border in the 1980s, smuggling has increased through the Caribbean and into the southeastern states. While much of the world's marijuana is actually produced in Jamaica, traffickers use other Caribbean islands as smuggling points.

As with Colombia, good international relations are vital for successful cooperation. One area of success has been the Bahamas, with the launch of Operation Bahamas and Turks and Caicos

Islands (OPBAT) in 1982. The DEA benefitted from its excellent relationships with the Commonwealth of the Bahamas and the Turks and Caicos islands (a dependent territory of Great Britain), helping their respective police forces patrol a daunting 100,000 square miles (259,067 sq km) of water surrounding 700 islands. Many of the traffickers have better resources than the islands' governments, including high-speed boats, seaplanes, and high-tech communications systems. They can also hide in Cuban air and sea space. The DEA's expertise and resources have been vital in helping these modest islands fight the drug war.

THE DEA IN EUROPE

The DEA enjoys excellent relations with many European governments, setting up permanent posts in those countries and launching complex cross-agency operations to trap drug lords. Many of these have included cooperation with the United Kingdom, Spain, and the European International Police Force (INTERPOL). In 1990, in line with its policy to hit drug lords where it hurts by seizing their assets, the DEA cooperated with British law-enforcement agencies to launch Operation Man on the British Isle of Man. The operation put agents on the inside of various money-laundering operations, with eye-opening results. The DEA seized a bank account containing $9 million, along with assets of $150 million from the "Bicycle Club" of California, probably the world's largest card casino. At one stage, the DEA bought 30 percent ownership of the club and watched in amazement as they received around $600,000 every month in profits.

DEA agents escort Fabio Ochoa, former right-hand man of notorious Colombian drug lord Pablo Escobar, following his extradition from Bogotá, Colombia, to Miami. This group was responsible for smuggling cocaine worth one million dollars to Europe and the United States every month.

THE DEA IN ASIA: THE GOLDEN TRIANGLE AND THE GOLDEN CRESCENT

Heroin starts life as the humble poppy plant, much of it grown in fields across southern Asia. Traditionally, it has been the "Golden Triangle" of Burma, Thailand, and Laos that has produced most of the world's heroin, with many farmers making it their sole crop

THE ESCAPADES OF ECSOBAR

The kingpin of the Medillin cartel was the infamous Pablo Escobar. He masterminded the 1989 bombing of an Avianca commercial airliner to kill two suspected informants on board; 110 passengers also died. After a lifetime of murder, mayhem, and running the most feared drug syndicate in history, he was captured by the CNP in June 1991, and locked up in Colombia's Envigado Jail. Such was his power, however, that he continued to run his drug empire from inside, even having the audacity to bury the bodies of two murdered associates in the prison grounds. Before he could be transferred to the high-security prison in Bogotá, he made a daring escape, apparently aided by several corrupt prison guards. He went on the run, and for the next 18 months, Escobar was the target of the biggest manhunt in Colombian history. The authorities finally got their man in December 1993, when Escobar was gunned down by the CNP in a standoff at his house in Medillin. His death also marked the death of his Medillin cartel.

because it is such a lucrative business.

In Burma, drug lord Khun Sa even bankrolled private armies to protect his $200-million fortune, and the authorities were powerless to stop him before the joint DEA-Burmese operation Tiger Trap finally smashed his empire in 1994. Drug syndicates were threatening to overwhelm the modest governments of those nations, and the DEA set up foreign offices and enforcement operations to crack down on heroin supply. It has had great success, and has also been

Pablo Escobar pictured with his wife Victoria in 1993. His days were already numbered: in December of that year, he was shot dead by Colombian police while on the run.

helped by a reduction in the number of heroin addicts at home.

But now a new source of heroin has emerged from Afghanistan, Pakistan, and Iran—known collectively as the "Golden Crescent." Although drugs were officially banned by the Taliban government of Afghanistan, much of their government's wealth seems to have come from Osama bin Laden's drug network. The growing of poppy crops was a strictly controlled business, but now, with the defeat of the Taliban, ordinary Afghans are starting to grow poppies

Here, a customs official displays almonds filled with heroin and marijuana in 2001. America faces a new drug wave from "The Golden Crescent" region—Afghanistan, Iran, and Pakistan.

independently, realizing they can make more money than from other cash crops. With the American involvement in Afghanistan and improved relations with Pakistan, it is hoped that the DEA can make some headway in reducing this new threat of cheap, high-grade heroin flooding the U.S. market. The U.S. and British governments are also seeking better relations with Iran, which could allow cooperation against drugs there, too.

But even where cooperation has been achieved, the difficulty for the DEA and host governments is in persuading local farmers to

PUTTING THE DRUG LORDS ON ICE

To seize the assets of international drug syndicates, the DEA launched a multinational sting in 1992 called Operation Green Ice. By now, the DEA had become so good at setting up fake money-laundering organizations that their newly created Trans America Ventures Associates (TARA) was named as one of the top 500 Hispanic corporations in America. The DEA used informants as go-betweens to establish links with the drug dealers, and offered to launder money anywhere in the world. The Colombian drug cartels took the bait, laundering over $20 million through TARA in Canada, the Caribbean, and Europe.

Encouraged by this success, the DEA expanded Green Ice, with international cooperation, into the Caymans, South America, Italy, Spain, and Great Britain, as well as at home. In 1992, Cali cartel bosses arrived in the United States, Europe, and South America for what they thought were routine business meetings. They got a shock: they were arrested.

In all, Green Ice captured seven Cali drug lords, 177 associates, and $50 million in cash and assets worldwide. Green Ice was the first international force to take on the financial assets of the Cali Mafia—and win.

stop growing drug crops and go back to growing food instead. Financial aid or farming subsidies may be the only way to do this in the short term. One Afghan farmer, interviewed by the BBC (British Broadcasting Corporation), summed up the problem: "We know it's wrong—we know where our poppy seeds end up. But I have to feed my family and there is nothing else here. If they want me to stop, they'll have to pay me as much as I get for my poppies, which is everything I have. Are they going to do that?"

HOW EUROPE FIGHTS XTC

The primary law-enforcement agency across Europe is Interpol, and by the late 1990s, it reported a massive increase in the production of the rave drug ecstasy, encouraged by the dance craze that swept across Europe and the United States.

Eighty percent of the world's ecstasy is made in secret laboratories in the Netherlands, with smaller amounts made in Belgium and elsewhere. European, African, and Asian drug syndicates then smuggle the drug out of the Netherlands into the rest of Europe and the world. Just like their Colombian counterparts, these traffickers are highly sophisticated, using all the latest technology to run their operations. Interpol, with the cooperation of European governments, has adopted various strategies to combat the epidemic.

They have established a database of all the logos used on ecstasy tablets to make identification easier during drug seizures. By 2000, over 500 logos were recorded, from doves to car emblems, like Mitsubishi, to designer clothing logos, like D&G (Dolce and Gabbana). They have also identified and destroyed laboratories where ecstasy tablets are made, thus disrupting and cutting off the supply of chemicals needed to make ecstasy.

By identifying and destroying the organizations behind the manufacture and supply of ecstasy and cooperating with European governments to build up intelligence on ecstasy smuggling, this leads to more arrests. Furthermore, by encouraging governments to enforce drug laws in their own countries and, in particular, to combat the use of drugs in nightclubs by persuading nightclub owners to adopt visible antidrug policies in their clubs, the soaring demand for the drug is reduced.

Many of Interpol's strategies are similar to the DEA's and have achieved great success. More than 14 million ecstacy tablets were

More than 200 million dollars' worth of opium, heroin, and marijuana go up in smoke as they are torched during an Interpol drug conference in Yangon, Myanmar (formerly Burma), in 1999. Many of Interpol's successful strategies mirror those of the DEA.

DRUGS MEAN TERRORISM—IT IS OFFICIAL

"If you quit drugs, you join the fight against terror in America," said President Bush, and it is true that the atrocities of September 11, 2001, were the responsibility of Al Qaeda, a terrorist network that gets much of its funding from its international drugs network. Considering that Americans spend a huge $60 billion a year on illegal drugs, Al Qaeda is potentially a rich organization. In response, the Office of National Drugs Control Policy (ONDCP) ran prime-time advertisements during the 2002 Super Bowl on February 3, 2002, which asked, "Where do terrorists get their money?" and explained that, "If you buy drugs, some of it might come from you."

According to the government, around half of the 28 terrorist organizations in the world are funded by drugs. For the first time, drug ads in America are showing young people the harm they can do others by buying drugs, not just to themselves. The message that drugs equal terrorism is getting through. Teenage focus groups who watched the ads showed "a strong decline in intention to use" drugs, said the ONDCP's education chief, Alan Levitt. Meanwhile, the war on drugs and terrorism continues.

Tragedy: the attack on the World Trade Center on September 11, 2001, established the first official link between drugs and terrorism.

French customs officials stand near plastic bags containing a part of a haul of 584,000 tablets of ecstasy seized in March 1999. The driver of a British-registered truck was stopped at the port of Dunkerque on his way to Britain. The truck also contained large quantities of cannabis and cocaine.

seized in Europe in 1999—three times the 1998 total—and 1.6 million of these were shipped to the United States.

Worldwide, 22 million tablets were seized in 1999, compared with 5.6 million the year before. Ecstasy is still a huge problem, but with the work of law enforcement agencies throughout the world and the ever-shifting pattern of drug culture, it is hoped that ecstasy use will soon decline.

DEA'S MOST WANTED

Many of the most-powerful drug traffickers are based in America's backyard, in Mexico and Colombia. Mexico has several independent drug syndicates, while many of Colombia's have organized under the umbrella of the North Valle cartel, which has largely taken over from the Medillin and Cali cartels of the past.

Make no mistake—those who profit from drugs are not the glamorous figures sometimes seen in movies. As William Ledwith, chief of DEA Office of International Operations, points out: "Today's organized crime leaders are strong, sophisticated, and destructive and have the capability of operating on a global scale. They are callous individuals who send their surrogates to direct distribution of the poison they ship to the United States. [They] are billionaires [whose] ultimate purpose is to amass large sums of money in order to maintain their obscene and lavish lifestyle free from the boundaries or confines of the law."

Here are some of the most infamous faces on the DEA's "Most Wanted" list.

Left: Drug cartels are often businesses run by families, because loyalty is everything for the man at the top. In many cases, the people who grow the crops and produce the raw materials for drug-making are small farmers from the poorer regions of Colombia.

MEXICO

The Amezcua-Contreras Organization

One of the most-powerful methamphetamine-smuggling syndicates, the organization is based in Guadalajara under the control of brothers Adan, Jesus, and Luis Amezcua-Contreras. The gang exploited a legal loophole in the drug laws to produce methamphetamine chemicals on a huge scale via the legitimate international chemical trade. The Mexican government finally arrested Jesus and Luis in June 1998, on provisional arrest warrants from the United States. The American request to extradite both for trial in the United States in 2001 was met halfway. Mexico agreed on Jesus (who quickly appealed and remains in Mexican custody), but denied extradition for Luis. Meanwhile, brother Adan served a two-year sentence in Mexico, and was released in May 1999.

The Caro-Quintero Organization

Originally part of the sinister Mexican Drug Trafficking Federation, the Caro-Quintero organization is run from Sonora, Mexico, by Miguel Caro-Quintero. It concentrates on trafficking huge amounts of marijuana and cocaine into the United States. Miguel's murderous brother Rafael previously headed the organization until his imprisonment for the killing of DEA Special Agent Enrique Camarena in Mexico in 1985. Miguel is high on the DEA's wanted list, and his case illustrates the importance of international cooperation for successful drug enforcement. He was captured in Mexico in 1992, but a Mexican judge dropped all charges and ordered his release. The Mexican government has since cooperated with the

A suspected drug dealer is arrested in Mexico City by a heavily armed special federal Mexican police officer in 2002. Cross-border cooperation boosts the DEA's chances of capturing the big drug producers and smugglers on their list.

DEA, agreeing in June 1999, that Miguel can be extradited to the United States on money-laundering charges if he is captured by Mexican police.

The Juarez Cartel

Formerly the most-powerful cartel in Mexico, this is run from its base in Juarez by Vicente Carillo-Fuentes, who eventually succeeded his brother Amado, who died during plastic surgery in 1997. The

consequences of Amado's death illustrate only too well the violence drugs can cause. The power vacuum left as a result of his death led to gang warfare on both sides of the Mexican border, killing traffickers and innocent men, women, and children alike, with 60 drug-related murders in just one year. Vicente is now wanted in Mexico and West Texas for running a continuing criminal enterprise in the region.

COLOMBIA

Although Mexican syndicates have recently begun production, Colombia remains the world's biggest producer and trafficker of cocaine. With the decline of the Cali cartel in the 1990s, other groups have seized their chance for power.

The Henao-Montoya Organization

Many drug mafia groups are based in the Northern Valle del Cauca region, among which the Henao-Montoya Organization is the most powerful. It is also one of the most violent in the world and was run by ruthless drug lord Jose Orlando Henao-Montoya until his arrest for money laundering and illicit earnings in September 1997. Jose got a taste of his own medicine in November 1998, when he was shot dead in the maximum-security wing of Bogotá Prison. His brother, Arcangel, took over his empire and remains a prime target

Left: A masked gunman of a Colombian drug gang in Medillin City, August 2000. The drug lords fight violent turf wars with private armies to establish their control over the drug trade.

Crop spraying has proved a highly effective way of destroying large coca plantations in Colombia, used for making cocaine. The less raw materials the drug lords have, the less drugs they can make.

for the DEA, both for drug trafficking and his links to terrorist groups aiming to destabilize the Colombian government.

The Urdinola-Grajales Organization

Another of the North Valle groups, this is run by Jairo Ivan and Julio Fabio Urdinola-Grajales, who are related to the Henao-Montoyas by marriage. Jairo was arrested in March 1994, on drug and murder charges, and his brother two years later. Although the murder charges were dropped, further drug charges were brought, and both remain in prison. Such is their power, however, that they continue to run their operation from inside.

The Diego-Montoya Organization

Diego's drug résumé is impressive—he was once a second lieutenant in the North Valle cartel, and now runs his own show, trafficking tons of cocaine every month from Mexico to the United States. Consequently, he is now one of the biggest cocaine producers and traffickers in Colombia, running supplies of cocaine base (unrefined cocaine) into Colombia from Peru and processing it at factories in the south.

The war on drugs is a real war. Here, a helicopter gunship patrols a known drug-producing area of Colombia to destroy drug crops and factories.

GOTCHA!

On March 9, 2002, Mexican police in Puebla, Mexico, captured the notorious Mexican drug lord, Benjamin Arellano-Felix of the AFO drug syndicate after a joint DEA-Mexican task force operation. After his capture, Benjamin confirmed that his

"Most wanted" drug baron Ramon Arellano Felix is killed in a gunfight with Mexican police on February 10, 2002. His brother Benjamin was captured the same day.

brother Ramon, the organization's chief enforcer, was killed in a shoot-out with Mexican police in Mazatlan, Mexico, on February 10, 2002. Benjamin had been on the DEA's "most wanted" list since 1992, and his capture was a major success for the DEA and the Mexican government. "This is a great day for law enforcement, the Mexican government, and citizens of the U.S.," said DEA Administrator Asa Hutchinson, recognizing the value of cross-border cooperation between the two countries. Since he was the head of one of the largest cocaine-smuggling rings in existence, Benjamin's capture is likely to severely reduce one of the main sources of cocaine into the United States. The DEA will now press for Benjamin to be extradited to face trial for his crimes in America.

The Chupeta Organization

Drug boss "Chupeta" (Juan Carlos Ramirez-Abadia) gave himself up to the CNP in March 1996, through fears for his safety from other drug lords and a knowledge that he would receive a more **lenient** sentence. He was sentenced to 24 years in prison, but due to his cooperation, may serve only one-third of that. He continues to influence the syndicate from inside, while leaving the day-to-day running to his associate "El Mono" (Jorge Orlando Rodriguez). Chupeta may consider his time inside a small price to pay for his crimes. He is worth an estimated $2.6 billion.

The Herrerra-Vasquez Organization

Based in Cali, Colombia, Hugo Herrera-Vasquez smuggles multi-ton shipments of cocaine into the United States via trafficking routes in Central America. He also runs a sophisticated money-laundering operation to receive the proceeds of his illegal cargo via the U.S. southwestern border area and Panama.

MEANWHILE, BACK HOME...

American James Joseph Bulger, known as "Whitey" on account of his silvery white hair, has the dubious honor of being on both the DEA's and the FBI's Top 10 Wanted Lists since 1995. Born in Boston, Bulger traffics drugs throughout the U.S. and Europe from bases in Colombia and Mexico. His reputation for violence is well founded—he is wanted for his part in 20 murders, and is known to carry weapons at all times. Among his other drug-related activities are **extortion** and money laundering.

THE DEA IN YOUR COMMUNITY

By the 1980s, around 1 in 10 Americans were thought to be using drugs regularly. The concern was that those drugs in demand were highly addictive—heroin and crack. The DEA realized that fighting the supply of drugs was not enough; they also had to reduce the demand.

The possibility that the United States might become a nation of addicts was all-too-real. Drug barons were targeting the poor and the young with cheap crack cocaine, and a new and terrifying concern emerged—"crack babies." They were given this name because they became addicted even before they were born because of their mothers smoking crack. The programs that the DEA implemented were much needed, and they are still in use today. They focus on three elements: education, rehabilitation, and regulation.

EDUCATION
The Demand Reduction Program (DRP)

Set up in 1986, the Demand Reduction Program is the DEA's foremost attempt to fight the demand for drugs alongside the supply. Experienced Special Agents are designated as Demand Reduction Coordinators (DRCs), who go into communities to work with local people by:

Left: Making the right choice: winning the war on drugs is just as much about reducing the demand for them as cutting off the supply.

- Increasing community awareness of the drug problem as a whole.
- Giving support to parents and educating them about the latest drug trends.
- Educating school children about the dangers of drugs.
- Helping employers and community leaders establish drug-free workplaces and run their own training programs to keep drugs out of the workplace.

As Special Agents, the DRCs provide a unique service to the community. They have a clear understanding of the drug situation overall and lots of experience working with law enforcement agencies, community leaders, schools, and employers. Their work reduces the demand for drugs, keeps cleaned-up communities from falling back into drug use again, and shrinks the power and wealth of the drug dealers on the streets. It also results in communities giving their wholehearted support to drug enforcement policies and the work of drug enforcement officers. The DRP is so successful that it is now a national DEA strategy.

MET IIs

As described, METs (Mobile Enforcement Teams) fight the supply of drugs in communities by breaking up drug gangs. DRCs designed the MET II program as a follow-up measure to help these newly cleaned-up communities stay that way.

MET IIs provide expert advice and training programs to show community leaders how to keep their neighborhood free from drugs. Around 50 MET II teams across 23 states are now active in the program.

Learning the lesson: the DEA's Demand Reduction Program includes DEA officers visiting schools regularly to educate school children about the dangers of drugs.

Drug Abuse Warning Network (DAWN)

The Drug Abuse Warning Network (DAWN) is a vital database of information and statistics on drug abuse in the United States published by the Department of Health and Human Services. It collects data from the emergency departments of hospitals and from medical examiners. The DEA uses many of its findings to educate local communities about the dangers of drugs.

Drug dealing and violent crime go hand in hand in our communities. As the MET teams clean out the dealers, so the violent crime disappears with them. By reducing drug abuse, we can also reduce the related violent crime.

Truth or Dare?

The DEA supports drug education programs in many community organizations, such as local Boys and Girls Clubs, Drug Abuse Resistance Education (DARE), and Law Enforcement Explorers, as well as schools and churches. Educating school children not to start taking drugs in the first place is one of the most essential parts of reducing the demand for drugs.

The Sports Drug Awareness Program (SDAP)

The DEA joined with the National High School Athletic Coaches Association in June 1984 to use high school athletes as positive role models for children. The DEA also managed to recruit several professional sports stars to spread the antidrug message. The program was a big success, as children sat up and took notice of their heroes' message that they should "Just Say No." The idea of using sports stars as role models against drugs continues today.

A Web of Support

The National Youth Antidrug Media Campaign, an organization aimed at helping youths ages 9–18 to reject drugs, and run by the Office of National Drug Control Policy, created a new Web site, theantidrug.com. This user-friendly, interactive site is for parents, teachers, and community leaders alike, offering excellent advice on how to keep their children drug-free. Created by leading experts in parenting and substance-abuse prevention, the site is an invaluable information center and provides a community where parents can come together and learn from each other.

REHABILITATION—KICKING THE HABIT

Drug education is great for persuading people not to start using drugs—but what about those already addicted, who have to discover a way of kicking the habit? They find it much harder to stop, because addictive drugs make the body crave the drug constantly. Heroin, in particular, causes serious withdrawal symptoms if addicts do not get their regular fix.

The DEA has encouraged drug rehabilitation centers and, in a nice twist, has often funded such programs using the money seized from drug dealers. In some areas, the DEA has even given houses seized from dealers back to the community and helped convert them into community and drug-rehabilitation centers.

REGULATION—KEEPING LEGAL DRUGS LEGAL

The DEA helps regulate the supply of controlled drugs to doctors and pharmacies. This means that those who need drugs like methadone (which helps people kick heroin) get them, while those who are simply trying to get their hands on cheap drugs to continue their habit do not.

A special division of the DEA, called Diversion Investigation, monitors how legal drugs and chemicals are transported and supplied throughout the United States to see whether these items are diverted from their legitimate use and into the manufacture of illegal drugs.

JOINING THE TEAM

You may want to consider joining the 9,000 men and women of the DEA when you finish your education. There are all sorts of roles to suit different people, from Special Agents to support staff. Here are the four main roles and the skills you need for them.

Special Agent

DEA Special Agents work on the frontline in the war against drugs, going undercover, carrying out surveillance, setting up antidrug

Just say no: Nancy Reagan, wife of former U.S. president Ronald Reagan, gets the message across to the community at an antidrug rally.

operations, arresting suspects, and testifying in court. It can be a difficult and dangerous job, but a rewarding one. Agents may work in the United States or abroad.

To qualify, you must be a U.S. citizen aged 21–33, with a valid driver's license. You need to be physically fit, with excellent hearing and vision. You also need a college degree with a cumulative GPA of 2.95 or higher. Depending on the actual role, you may need additional skills and experience, such as foreign languages, or technical and administrative skills. For further details, call Special Agent Recruitment at 1-800-DEA-4288. There may be a DEA field office near you that you can visit, too.

Intelligence Research Specialist

The specialist's role is to gather and analyze all kinds of intelligence about drug-trafficking organizations, such as drug manufacture, trafficking routes, and how the organization operates. The specialist then presents this information to Special Agents and in court, as evidence in drug enforcement cases. They may be assigned to

Drug counseling by specialist Demand Reduction Coordinators gives these kids a goal in life and teaches them to put their families first. Problems with drugs are often caused by problems at school or at home—drug users need to straighten out their lives as well in the battle to kick the habit.

JUSTICE FOR ALL

The DEA's Office of Training is at the new Justice Training Center in Quantico, Virginia, which officially opened on April 28, 1999. It provides training for all Special Agents, intelligence specialists, Diversion Investigators, forensic chemists, and support staff. Recruits undergo different training programs depending on which post they are joining. For example, Special Agents receive rigorous physical training and learn surveillance and asset-seizure techniques. Forensic chemists, on the other hand, learn laboratory techniques. But all recruits, whatever their role, are given thorough training in how the DEA operates and how to deal with the moral dilemmas of the job—how to react to bribery attempts by drug dealers, for example. The center also runs specialized courses for other local and federal law-enforcement agencies. From the start, the Justice Training Center equips our dedicated law enforcement agencies with the skills to do the best job possible.

specialist duties at home or abroad, in field offices, at EPIC, or at the DEA's Intelligence Division headquarters in Arlington, Virginia.

Training is given through a six-week program, where new intelligence recruits are taught how the DEA operates and how to gather and analyze information. On graduating from the program, they will work with experienced specialists until they are ready to work on their own. They must also be willing to work anywhere in the world. For more information, call Intelligence Specialist Recruitment at 202-307-4088 or visit your nearest DEA office.

Hands up who hates drugs. The police and the DEA work hard in our classrooms to get the antidrug message across to kids. It is far easier not to take drugs in the first place than try and kick the habit later on, once you are trapped in an addiction.

Forensic Chemist

If you are fascinated by science at school, this could be the job for you. After a five-week training program, you will be working in state-of-the-art laboratories, analyzing all sorts of evidence, from drugs to fingerprints. You will also be carrying out research to find new ways to analyze evidence and providing vital information on drug-trafficking techniques.

Qualifications

A scientific background is useful, and you must be willing to work anywhere in the United States. After completing a training program that teaches you how to handle and analyze evidence, identify drugs, and carry out research, you will complete a one-year probationary period before you become a fully qualified forensic chemist.

The DEA campaigns tirelessly in our communities to remove scenes like this from our streets—and maybe you could be part of the team when you leave school or college.

As a forensic chemist with the DEA, you will examine and analyze drugs like cocaine in order to build a court case that brings drug dealers to justice.

Diversion Investigator

This role is about investigating the diversion, by individuals and organizations, of legal chemicals and drugs into illegal usage, such as the manufacture of methamphetamines.

You need to be physically fit, with excellent hearing and vision. Technical and administrative skills are useful. You will undergo an 11-week training program at the Diversion Investigator Training School to learn how the DEA operates and how to identify and analyze diversion techniques. On graduating from training school, you must be willing to work anywhere in the world.

Party on, but keep it drug free! You do not need drugs to have a good time and enjoy yourself. Get the message across to your family and friends.

GLOSSARY

Addict: someone who is physically or psychologically dependent on a drug

Amphetamine: a chemical that causes stimulation of the central nervous system

Anesthetic: a substance that produces loss of sensation with or without loss of consciousness

Asset: an item of value owned by a person

Asset forfeiture: legally seizing the assets of a drug dealer to prevent him from funding further drug-trafficking operations

Cartel: a combination of groups with a common action or goal

Cocaine: made from the leaves of the coca plant, this is a stimulant, making users feel more alert

Ecstasy: a hallucinogenic drug taken in pill form

Euphoria: a feeling of well-being or elation

Extortion: the act of obtaining money or other property from a person by means of force or intimidation

Extradite: to surrender an alleged criminal from one state or nation to another having jurisdiction to try the charge

Hallucination: a state of consciousness in which a person imagines he or she is seeing things, people, or shapes that are not actually there

Hallucinogen: a mind-altering drug, such as LSD, that affects the user's ability to see colors, shapes, and depth

Heroin: a depressant that relaxes the user, this is made from the opium poppy

Infiltrate: to enter or become established in gradually or unobtrusively, usually for subversive purposes

Lenient: lesser; indulgent

LSD: Lysergic Acid Diethylamide—a hallucinogenic drug taken in pill form

Marijuana: made from the seeds and dried leaves of the cannabis plant, this is a depressant, making the user feel more relaxed

Racketeering: the act of practicing extortion

Solvent: something that dissolves another substance

Sting: a plan implemented by undercover police in order to trap criminals

Trafficking: smuggling illegal drugs from one location to another with the purpose of selling them

CHRONOLOGY

1970: Controlled Substances Act (CSA) is passed, creating a comprehensive drug-classification system for the first time.

1973: President Nixon creates the DEA as the nation's premier drug enforcement agency.

1974: EPIC, the DEA's intelligence center, is established at El Paso.

1979: Drug abuse reaches a peak in the United States—10 percent of Americans admit to regular drug use; cocaine is the decade's drug of choice; the Domestic Cannabis Eradication and Suppression Program (DCE/SP) is launched to wipe out America's only home-grown illegal drug.

1980: Operation Swordfish is launched in Florida to trap drug lords in a money-laundering sting.

1981: Estimates suggest heroin availability in the United States has been reduced by a record 40 percent since 1976, but crack cocaine is becoming the new menace.

1984: Operation Pipeline is launched to tackle the huge amounts of drugs and cash transported along U.S. highways.

1988: A record 132,276 lb (60,000 kg) of crack is seized in the United States; crack use becomes America's worst drug epidemic in history.

1991: The largest seizure of heroin in U.S. history is made, when 1,000 lb (494 kg) of the drug is found in San Francisco, smuggled in from Taiwan.

1992: The DEA receives its first billion-dollar budget; the "kingpin" strategy is launched to take down the bosses of organized crime by smashing their trafficking infrastructure and seizing their assets.

1993: The notorious Colombian drug lord Pablo Escobar is shot dead by Colombian police in a gun battle following the biggest manhunt in Colombian history.

1993–1998: Rave dance culture hits the United States; use of the rave drug ecstasy increases 500 percent.

1994: METs (Mobile Enforcement Teams) are established to tackle drug-related violence in communities.

1997: NDPIX (National Drug Pointer Index) is set up to alert agents to possible duplicate enforcement operations around the country.

2001: Former U.S. Attorney and congressman Asa Hutchinson becomes DEA Administrator.

2002: Mexican drug boss Benjamin Arellano Felix is finally captured in Mexico after 10 years on the DEA's "most wanted" list; his brother Ramon is killed in a shoot-out by Mexican police.

FURTHER INFORMATION

For information on working for the DEA, contact your nearest DEA laboratory for more details:

Mid-Atlantic Laboratory, Washington, D.C. 20532-001

NE Laboratory, New York, 10011

North Central Laboratory, Chicago, Illinois, 60605

South Central Laboratory, Dallas , Texas, 75235

SE Laboratory, Miami, Florida, 33166

SW Laboratory National City, California, 91950

USEFUL WEB SITES

For the DEA: www.dea.gov

For the Department of Justice: www.usdoj.gov

For the FBI: www.fbi.gov

For an antidrug Web site, see the Office of National Drug Control Policy, at: www.theantidrug.com

Drug Abuse Warning Network (DAWN):
www.samhsa.gov/oas/dawn.htm

For the National Youth Antidrug Media Campaign:
www.mediacampaign.org

FURTHER READING

Bowden, Mark. *Killing Pablo: The Hunt for the World's Greatest Outlaw*. New York: Atlantic Monthly Press, 2001.

DEA Staff. *DEA Undercover*. New York: St Martin's Press, 1999.

Greene, Meg (editor: Arthur M. Schlesinger). *The Drug Enforcement Administration*. New York: Chelsea House Publishers, 2001.

Levine, Michael. *Deep Cover: How to Take Back Your Neighborhood, Schools, and Families from Drug Dealers*. New York: Dell Books, 1991.

Levine, Michael. *Fight Back: The Inside Story of How DEA Infighting, Incompetence, and Subterfuge Lost Us the Biggest Battle of the Drug War*. New York: Doubleday, 1990.

Streatfeild, Dominic. *Cocaine: An Unauthorised Biography*. London: Virgin, 2001.

ABOUT THE AUTHOR

Clive Somerville is a freelance writer and editor. After completing a politics degree, he wrote and recorded features for BBC radio before setting off on a "short trip" to see the world. He returned two years later, joined the editorial team of a publishing firm, and has been writing ever since. He has recently written pocket guides to the Internet and PCs, contributed to the British *Sunday Times Guide to Education Online*. He has also written and edited articles for some of the best-selling educational partworks around the world. He lives and works in the UK.

INDEX

References in italics refer to illustrations